I0209379

Nicholas Vansittart

An Inquiry Into the State of the Finances of Great Britain

In answer to Mr. Morgan's Facts

Nicholas Vansittart

An Inquiry Into the State of the Finances of Great Britain
In answer to Mr. Morgan's Facts

ISBN/EAN: 9783337062767

Printed in Europe, USA, Canada, Australia, Japan

Cover: Foto ©Suzi / pixelio.de

More available books at **www.hansebooks.com**

AN
INQUIRY
INTO THE
STATE
OF THE
FINANCES OF GREAT BRITAIN;
IN
ANSWER
TO
Mr. MORGAN's FACTS.

By NICHOLAS VANSITTART, Esq.

LONDON:
PRINTED FOR J. OWEN, NO. 168, PICCADILLY.

M.DCC.XCVI.

INQUIRY, &c.

ABOUT two years ago I had occasion, in answer to the gloomy predictions of JASPER WILSON, to take a cursory view of the resources of the Nation, and to examine the general state of its Commerce and Finances. I then endeavoured to shew " on how vain a foundation the fears of the desponding rested," and the events of the momentous and important period which has since elapsed, had in my opinion so

proved

proved .the correctness of my statements, and the justice of my conclusions, that I little expected to have been again called upon to defend them. A work however has lately appeared, not in the form of a Newspaper Essay, or an anonymous Pamphlet, but of a grave discussion, the avowed production of a Gentleman of acknowledged talents, and who may even rank very high among *Statesmen*, if his own definition of the sciences of Government and Finance be just---*that the one requires only a little Common Sense, and the other only a little common Arithmetic.* In that work, supported by the authority of Mr. Morgan's name, and impressed on the public attention by the solemnity of its title, " *Facts addressed to the serious attention of the People of Great Britain*," the same strain prevails, of lamentation and despondence, which distinguished Jasper Wilson's florid declamations. *Facts* are always valuable, but I believe the real *facts* to be widely different from

Mr.

Mr. Morgan's statement; and I should lament on much better grounds than any concern for my reputation as an Author, if such *facts* were true, as the inevitable Bankruptcy and approaching ruin of my Country.

Mr. Morgan declines entering into any inquiry as to the justice and necessity of the War, though it seems reasonable to have entered into some such inquiry before he charged the Ministry * with *error*, *misconduct*, *wickedness* and *incapacity*. But as I have already laid my opinion on those points before the Public, I can have no objection now to follow his example, in separating them from the present discussion. He likewise declines "entering into a description of the carnage and miseries by which this War has been so peculiarly distinguished, and which must sicken every friend of humanity, well knowing that considerations

* See Preface to Facts, &c.

of

of this kind seldom influence the Coun-
cils of Statesmen, or even sufficiently
rouse the indignation of a People, who,"
he observes, " do not begin seriously to
feel for the miseries of their fellow-crea-
tures, till misfortune presses immediately
on themselves." After thanking Mr.
MORGAN, in the name of the Nation, for
his compliment to our Benevolence, I
shall dismiss this subject also, because I
believe the true authors of the carnage
and miseries are sufficiently known and
detested already.

Having just hinted at these prelimina-
ry points in his Preface, he observes (in
his second page), that the warmest advocates for the War, acknowledge its
prospect at present to be neither encou-
raging nor consolatory. On this part of
the subject, he says he feels no disposi-
tion to enter ; though he cannot forbear
slightly recurring to it afterwards, and
asking (p. 11), " whether our Debts
have

have been compensated by the value of our Conquests in Corsica, Isle Dieu, and *elsewhere ?*" It may be remarked, that *elsewhere* is a word of comprehensive meaning; and includes Martinique, Tobago, all the principal Posts in St. Domingo, the French Settlements on the Continent of India, Malacca, Cochin, Ceylon, and the Cape of Good Hope. But as I never attempted, nor wished to defend the War on account of the advantages of Conquest, and as Mr. MORGAN declares his design is not to examine the operations of the *War* Minister, but those of the Minister of *Finance*, I shall confine myself to the same line of discussion.

Mr. MORGAN enters upon his principal subject by observing, that " it is a melancholy truth, that every War in which we have been engaged for the last century, has uniformly been more expensive than any that had preceded it."

It

It is certain that the expences of War,
like all other expences, must increase in
proportion to the advanced price of those
articles which the Government is obliged
to purchase*; and it is no more possible
for the Government, than for an indivi-
dual, to maintain any Establishment now,
on the same income which was sufficient
to support it a certain number of years
ago. Mr. MORGAN proceeds to observe,
" that the American War was considered
" as having reached the highest point of
" profusion; and that neither the Credit
" nor the Resources of the Nation (p. 3),
" could survive a repetition, much less
" an aggravation, of the evil: but that
" the experience of the three last years
" had shewn, that the limits of our Ex-
" penditure were at a much greater dis-
" tance, than the extravagance even of

* Naval Stores are at this time, on the whole, considerably more than 35l. per cent. higher than in the American
War; and Victualling Stores have probably risen in their
price in a still greater proportion. Ship-building has
increased about 15l. per cent.

" that

" that War had taught us to place them.
" Of this fact no doubt can be entertain-
" ed by any person who is the least ac-
" quainted with Public Affairs; and the
" following Statements are given, not
" with the view of proving what is al-
" ready so well known, but in order to
" point out the enormous magnitude of
" the sum by which the Expences of the
" four first years of the present, have ex-
" ceeded those of the same term in the
" American War."

At the hazard of being considered by
Mr. MORGAN as a person not the least
acquainted with Public Affairs, I venture
not only to doubt, but to deny these assertions; appealing at the same time to his
candour, whether it be fair to bring the
years 1776 and 1777, in which we were
only engaged in a contest with our American Colonies, whose Revolt was then
unsupported by any Foreign Power, into
comparison with the exertions of the present

sent War? In 1776, only 10,000 additional Seamen were voted; and so small an increase of expence was thought necessary, that it appears by Mr. Morgan's own statement (page 14), that the Sum borrowed did not exceed 1,827,500l. In 1777, the Contest beyond the Atlantic became more alarming in its appearance; but it was not till about the middle of 1778 that Hostilities with France commenced. The first Campaign of the present War began as early in the year as the month of February; but on that circumstance I shall lay no stress. I am willing to enter into a fair comparison of the Expences of the four years, commencing with 1778, and of the four years, commencing with 1793, arguing on a supposition that the Expences of the present year are provided for. I have in Table I. stated the Estimates of each year; but I shall by no means admit that a fair comparison can from thence be formed of the actual Expence in the two periods.

In

In the American War the Floating Debt of the Navy and Ordnance accumulated in an irregular manner, and the deficiencies of one year not being provided for in the next, the Unfunded Debt increased by the end of the War to the immense extent of twenty-seven millions*. In the present War, all the Extraordinary Expences of every year, as far as they could be ascertained, have been carried to account in the next Supply, so that no accumulation of Unfunded Debt has been suffered to remain, beyond the ascertained and avowed amount for which Taxes have been provided. I shall not here enter into any detail of the various benefits resulting from this excellent arrangement.---
They are indeed sufficiently obvious to every one who considers the advantage of going to market with ready money, instead of paying in Promissory Notes, at a considerable discount. I shall only observe, that adding to the Estimates

The exact sum was 26,867,993l.

the

the increase of Navy Debt and Ordnance
Debentures incurred in the American
War, and a fair proportion of the
Floating Debt unprovided for at the
close of that War, the amount will be
found to exceed the largest statement
of the Expences of the present War.
Leaving this statement without further
comment, I shall proceed to consider
the amount of the Debt incurred in
the present War. This Mr. MORGAN
represents as more than *double* the Debt
incurred during the same period, in the
most expensive War that had ever been
carried on by this Country. Table II.
will shew the exact amount of the
Funds created during the periods we are
comparing, the Annuities being included in both. Here Mr. MORGAN attempts to add the Imperial Loan,
as if a possible eventual charge was
to be considered as a debt incurred
in the first instance. Except protesting
against this doctrine of Mr. MORGAN's,
that the *Surety for a Debt* is the *immediate*
Debtor,

Debtor, I do not much differ from this part of his account. But his statement of the Unfunded Debt is of a singular nature indeed: In this instance his Fancy had more room to display itself, and he has given it full scope. With regard to the Debt of the present War, on the first article I have only to observe, that the five millions of Navy Debt are intended to be funded, and that there exist adequate Funds for defraying the Interest, so that they only differ from a Funded Debt in not being regularly reduced into Stock. The next article is a curious one, " Vote of Credit---four millions." 2,500,000l. were indeed raised by a Vote of Credit last year, and provided for in the Supplies in December, so that they are no longer any *debt*, and the other 1,500,000l. to the best of my knowledge, never had any existence at all. The next article even improves upon this; it is a debt of " one million not paid by the East India Company, but taken as part of the Supplies in 1794 and 1795." The Govern-

ment

ment not receiving this sum, to which it was entitled, was obliged to raise the Money by other means, and it still continues due ; so that instead of a Debt, it is actually a Credit, which I have no doubt the Government will sooner or later realize. The last article is that of Exchequer Bills ; but as 5,500,000l. were kept circulating in time of Peace, it is only the amount exceeding that sum, which can be considered as a debt occasioned by the War; so that Mr. MORGAN's Budget of

$£.$ 16,000,000

Is filled up by		
Debt already provided for	-	$£.$ 5,000,000
Imaginary Debt	- -	9,500,000
Actual Credit	- -	1,000,000

$£.$ 15,500,000

Which leaves the Excess of real Unfunded Debt no more than - - * $£.$ 500,000

This statement requires no observations, nor is it easy to make such upon it as are consistent with my respect for Mr. MORGAN. But in his improved Edition he so far attempts to account for it,

* Which is the Excess of Exchequer Bills, including the Vote of Credit, beyond those issued and usually circulated in time of Peace.

as

as to enumerate a variety of articles,
which he says " may not only be placed
" against the Unfunded Debt incurred
" previous to Hostilities, but so far ex-
" ceed it-as to carry the Expence of the
" War to one hundred millions, exclu-
" sive of the Imperial Loan." The only
real article *unprovided* for, of those included in his enumeration, is 1,500,000L
Navy Debt, incurred beyond the sum intended to be funded, to which I will add,
for the sake of a clear view of the total
Expence, 2,500,000l., which has been
stated as likely to be added to the Navy
Debt in the course of the year. I will
further allow between five and six millions for future miscellaneous and extraordinary Expences. As to the new
imaginary articles by which he supports
his old ones, I shall leave them to share
the same fate, and only observe, that
the utmost Expence, as far as it can yet
be foreseen, will not exceed at the end of
this year, sixty-five, or at the utmost
seventy millions. If the *Expences of the
War* mean the *Money* spent in it, as Com-

.mon

mon Sense seems to require, he must re-
sort to his fund of *imaginary* articles, for
five and thirty, or at least thirty millions,
to make up his calculation.*　But if in
defiance of the common meaning of
words, Mr. MORGAN intends to state all
the Stock created in the War as so much
money actually expended, his exagger-
ations will *only* amount to about twelve
millions.

And this naturally leads me to consider
the Loans raised in each period, with a
general view of the National Debt, and
to examine the plan adopted for its
reduction.

* The money raised by Loans during the
　War, amounts to　-　-　£.51,500,000
The Navy Debt funded in 1794 and 1795,　-　3,536,422
Navy Debt about to be funded,　-　5,000,000
Further increase of Navy Debt,　-　1,500,000
Expected increase of ditto within the year,　2,500,000
Increase of Exchequer Bills,　-　-　500,000
　　　　　　　　　　　　　　　　£. 64,536,422
Allow for possible Excess, for Contingencies,
　and Extraordinaries, to 31st Dec. 1796,　-　5,463,578
　　　　　　　　　　　　　　　　£. 70,000,000

It

It has always been a favourite amuse-
ment, and sometimes an useful occupa-
tion, of men versed in calculation, to
speculate on subjects of Finance. The
infallible schemes devised by young Politicians for paying off the National
Debt, are as numerous as the impreg-
nable Fortresses traced on paper by
young Engineers : nor have I any doubt,
that of the 36,000 plans lately laid before the French Committee of Finance,
for redeeming the Assignats, a great number appeared demonstrably true to their
inventors, and extremely plausible to
those who took them into consideration.
But one is naturally unwilling to believe
that VAUBAN has built on a false foundation, or that Dr. PRICE, and the *heir*
of his talents and his principles, have calculated on fallacious grounds. Espe-
cially when one considers the magisterial
consequence with which they pronounce
their Decrees, and the dignified authority with which Ministers are arraigned
for not attending sufficiently to their
suggestions. Yet I am compelled to observe,

serve, that these Gentlemen seem to have contented themselves with speculations in their closets, without much inquiry among men of business, into the practicability of executing their plans. It no doubt arises from this abstraction from the affairs'of common life, and not from any wilful misrepresentation, that Mr. MORGAN, blaming Mr. PITT for borrowing on terms less favourable to the Public than his Predecessor in Office, selects as a fair comparison, four years in which only 14,760,000l. were raised by Loans, to oppose to four in which 51 millions and a half have been borrowed. I shall therefore take the same four years of the American War, of which I have already stated the Expences; not because they are more favourable to my argument, but because they are more just; for I shall presently shew, that they are much less favourable than a fair comparison would require. Table III. shews the Money borrowed, and the Stock created during the two periods

I have

I have compared, by which it appears
that Lord NORTH, for thirty-seven millions borrowed, gave upwards of fifty-
seven millions of Stock : Mr. PITT, for
something less than fifty-four millions
nine hundred thousand pounds, gave
only seventy-eight millions ; so that,
according to Mr. MORGAN's method
of calculation, the larger sum was borrowed on more favourable terms than
the smaller, by about six millions. One
of our most distinguished Statesmen dif-
fers indeed so totally from Mr. MORGAN's
ideas, as to have stated his opinion, that
the Capital Stock created is a matter of
perfect indifference, and that the only
circumstance to be attended to, is the Interest paid. The same Table will shew
the rate of Interest on each of the
Loans in these periods ; and the result
of my comparison will be no less satis-
factory to Mr. Fox than Mr. MORGAN.

The average rate of Interest from 1778
to 1781, was - - - - £.5 13 5½
That of the Loans during the present War 4 10 9½

Difference in favour of the present War - £.1 2 8

D   It

It is necessary to remark, in order to prevent any mistake that might arise from inattention to this circumstance, that in the years of the American War to which I refer, the Lottery was given as a part of the bonus to the Subscribers to the Loan; I have therefore considered the profit arising from the Lottery, as so much additional Principal, the Interest of which, as making a part of the Interest of the Loan, is brought to account in Table III. before referred to. In the present War, the Lottery having been applied to other public purposes, does not produce any addition of the same sort. I must likewise observe, that I by no means intend in this comparison to censure Lord NORTH, who probably did the best the situation of Public Credit then admitted; but I must nevertheless maintain, that the terms of the late Loans, considering they were contracted at a time when the National Debt was increased near 100 millions, are

a de-

a decisive proof either of extraordinary prosperity in the State, or ability
in the Minister. Mr. MORGAN, however, exclusive of all comparisons,
criticizes the Loans of the present
War very severely, and not content
with censuring them, he foresees much
worse to come. With his future Loans,
the mere phantoms of his imagination, I can have nothing to do, but
with regard to the one last contracted,
I am sure Mr. MORGAN cannot have
conversed with any man of business. He
takes it for granted that Mr. PITT could
have made this at the rate of 120l.
of 4l. per cent. Stock, for every 100l.
borrowed; that is, that instead of the
*present principal and interest, and a bonus
which he estimates at* 7l. 13s. 8d. half-
penny, the Lenders would have agreed
to 8s. 6d. *per cent. more interest,* 25 *per
cent. less capital, and no bonus at all.*
When Mr. MORGAN produces the list
of Bankers that would have subscribed

to

to such a Loan, it will be time enough to discuss the merits of it with him.

As the last Loan is the only one which Mr. MORGAN has chosen to examine, I shall now proceed in his own order, to inquire into the total amount of the National Debt. The general account of the Funded Debt on the 5th of January, 1796, without making any deduction for what has been purchased by the Commissioners for reducing the National Debt, amounts to---

Stock created before	Principal.	Interest.	Management.
Jan. 5, 1784 -	£.211,363,254	7,937,231	107,824
Between Jan. 5, 1784, and Jan. 5, 1788 -	26,867,993	1,209,939	12,950
Since Jan. 5, 1788	47,536,423	2,284,209	25,204
In 1796 * - -	26,100,000	783,000	11,745
	£.311,847,670	12,214,379	157,723

* There is no account of this yet in the Exchequer, but it must be nearly as here stated.

To

To this should be added five millions of Navy Debt provided for, but not yet funded; 500,000l. increase in Exchequer Bills; 1,500,000l. Navy Debt already incurred; and 2,500,000l. estimated for the Expences of the present year, which will complete the view of the public incumbrances beyond the Floating Debt in time of Peace, except as far as any increase may arise from Extraordinary Expences not yet ascertained.

In this Statement, the Annuities of all kinds are included in the Interest, as being periodical yearly payments, but not in the Principal: in the first place, because they will expire of themselves after a certain time; and secondly, because they have no precise and definite Capital.

Mr. MORGAN, by calculating the value of the Annuities, increases the Capital of the Debt about twenty-five millions.---
His

His calculations are of an unfavourable
kind, but I shall not dispute them, as I
admit the Annuities to be a *real* part of
the Debt, though not capable of being
reduced to any exact Capital; but he
goes a great way farther, adding above
eighteen millions more for the *imaginary*
Debt of which I have spoken before. As
Mr. MORGAN refers back to his former
Statement of that subject, I shall content myself with referring back to mine.

The correcting his Accounts would not
essentially have lessened the pathos of his
succeeding lamentations; I cannot therefore but wish Mr. MORGAN had so far re-
garded his character as a Calculator, as
not to fall into an error of 18 millions
Sterling. But what I most object to in
these lamentations is, that he points out
no remedy for the evils which he de-
plores. He tells us, indeed, "that this
" Country has the greatest reason to *la-*
" *ment,* or rather to *execrate* these mea-
" sures,

" sures, which have so often interrupted
" its peace for the last Century." But
as he does not tell us what those measures
were, I am perfectly at a loss *what to ex-*
ecrate, and possibly might fix upon objects very different from those which Mr.
MORGAN has in view.

Mr. MORGAN here enters into a speculation upon the future Peace Establishment, and the Rental of the Kingdom.
As our business is with *Facts*, I shall not
follow him farther in this loose and uncertain speculation, than just to state my
opinion (not wholly unfounded), that he
is mistaken to the amount of some hundred thousands pounds a-year, in the
first Article, and at least ten millions in
the second.

I am now come to the consideration
of the plan adopted for redeeming the
National Debt ; and having before stated
its total amount, shall now mention the
sum bought up by the Commissioners.

The

The total Capital of the Debt is - £. * 311,847,670
Value of the Annuities, according to Mr.
  Morgan - - - 24,730,269
Unfunded Debt, including what is ex-
  pected within the year - - - 9,500,000
                  £. 346,077,939
Stock redeemed by the Commissioners - 18,001,655
                  £. 328,076,284

But as every Reader must be struck with the enormous difference between Mr. MORGAN's total and mine, it is necessary to enter into some explanation of it. A part arises from his bringing in his Imaginary Debt. But the great difference (no less than fifty millions) arises from his converting sixty-three millions of 5 and 4 per cents. and near 1,700,000l. a year in Annuities at one stroke into 3 per cent. Stock. Mr. MORGAN expresses so much indignation at every Minister who borrows in a 3 per Cent. Fund, that I little suspected he would execute that which the worst of Ministers, in the worst of times, has never thought of. Mr.

* Supposing the Debt of this year as stated in p. 20.

MORGAN

MORGAN says this is done to give an accurate account of the Debt.---How an account is to be rendered *accurate* by making it *false*, I am at a loss to guess. If it is by way of computing the progress made by the Commissioners in redeeming the Debt, the reasoning fails equally, for as the 4 and 5 per Cents. are redeemable at par, as well as the 3 per Cents. the Sinking Fund, when applied to their reduction, will extinguish them as fast, and even according to Mr. MORGAN's calculation, much faster; making no allowance at all for his fifty millions of additional Capital. I particularly wish him to take some opportunity of stating his reason for making the Debt appear so much larger than it really is: only one occurs to me, and that I never can suspect to be the true one, because it would be as little reconcileable to *common honesty*, as the account itself is to *common sense* or *common arithmetic.*

E

Here

Here Mr. MORGAN is so terrified at the dreadful phantom he has conjured up, that he sinks into the lowest despondency; and after reckoning up the wars and rumours of war which this century has produced already, dooms us to warfare, bankruptcy and ruin in times to come.

That a great part of this century has been spent in war, I am ready with Mr. MORGAN to regret, but my observations on the subject have only led to one general conclusion---that Peace has always continued longer in proportion as *France* was left in an *exhausted state at the conclusion of the War*. Thus the Peace of Paris lasted considerably longer than that of Aix-la-Chapelle; and that of Utrecht, which was concluded when France was on the eve of bankruptcy, was by far the longest as well as most secure in this century. Whether this observation can lead to any just conclusions as to the permanence

manence of a future Peace, I am far from taking upon myself to decide.

But instead of dwelling longer on this subject, I shall proceed to consider the effects of the system established for reducing the National Debt. "The plan "(says Mr. Morgan), which the Chan- "cellor of the Exchequer has adopted "for redeeming the National Debt, is " well known to have been one of the " three which at his request were com- "municated to him by Dr. Price in the "year 1786, and though originally the "weakest of the three, was not only mu- "tilated and enfeebled by his alterations "at its first establishment, but rendered "still more ineffectual by subsequent ne- "glect and mismanagement." It here is necessary to make a few remarks upon the plans alluded to, as they are stated in Mr. Morgan's Review of Dr. Price's Writings on Finance ; not with an intention of investigating them thoroughly, which would require a good deal of lei-

sure

sure and much intricate calculation; but of obviating the natural conclusion, that the Minister must necessarily be wrong in adopting the weakest of the plans, and still more so in mutilating it. On the two not adopted I shall only observe at present, that whatever might be their merit in other respects, they required an addition of 600,000l. a year in new taxes to be imposed within five years. This was thought improper, if not impracticable, at that time (1786) by the Minister; more so I believe by the Nation, but most of all by Dr. Price and Mr. Morgan themselves, who have contended ever since, that the Revenue was above a million yearly deficient; so that to have executed either of these plans, new Taxes must annually have been imposed to the amount of at least 1,600,000l. The third plan (which however was no new invention or discovery, being nothing more than a calculation of the effect of applying a million annually in the purchase of Stock) was in sub-

stance

stance adopted, but some alterations were
made, which entitle it, in Mr. MORGAN's
opinion, to no better terms than *mutilated,
impotent and defective*; yet he is never
more vehement on any occasion than in
the reproaches he addresses to Mr. PITT,
for not attributing the merit of this impotent plan to Dr. PRICE. Surely if
Mr. PITT spoiled the plan, he made it his
own, and it would have been an injustice
to Dr. PRICE to make him pass for the
Author of it. Before I examine the effect which this *mutilated* plan, under Mr.
PITT's *negligent and unskilful management*,
has produced, I must state a few general
observations on the subject. The Calculators of plans for reducing the National Debt, never attend to any thing
but the quickest possible means of pay-
ment. As *Calculators*, they do right;
but when they arraign Ministers with
such dogmatical haughtiness for not
following their systems, it is proper to
ask if an enlightened Minister has not
some other considerations to attend to.
The

The National Debt is indeed, in *one* point of view, a charge upon the general mass of National Property, which is defrayed by deducting a certain portion of every man's income by means of taxation: In *another*, it constitutes the property, and furnishes the income of a great and respectable class of the Inhabitants of the Country: In a third, it is a deposit for Capital not otherwise employed.

The extinction of the Debt is not, however, by any means the only purpose which the Redeeming Fund is found to answer: it regulates in a considerable degree the ordinary rate of Interest, and the general state of Credit as well *private* as *public*. By producing a regular and steady supply of money in the market, it prevents great and sudden fluctuations, and counteracts fraudulent combinations to influence the price of Stock. That these are objects of great importance in a Commercial Country, Mr. Morgan will

not

not deny ; nor has he attempted to shew,
that in any of these points of view it has
proved impotent and defective.

Of its effect in supporting Public Credit, no stronger evidence can be given,
than the comparison before stated of the
Loans in the last War and the present :
it will be difficult otherwise to account for
the reduced rate of Interest at which the
Money has been obtained. If this be
true (and I only give it as a conjecture
on which every Reader will form his own
conclusion), the Public are indebted to
Mr. PITT's *mutilated* plan for saving a
perpetual Annuity of £. 585,812, worth,
at 4 per cent.* a capital of 14,646,312l.
But how far Mr. PITT has mutilated Dr.
PRICE's plan, with regard even to the Redemption, appears from a comparison of
the first seven years of the calculation in
Mr. MORGAN's book, with the sum ac-

* I consider 4 per Cent. as nearly the general average
of Interest in a series of years.

tually

tually redeemed by the Commissioners,
which was,   - -   £. 10,109,400
The sum, as calculated by

    Dr. PRICE   - -   9,112,705

Balance in favour of the
  actual payments,   -   £.996,695

And, if the comparison was carried
down to the present time, its result would
be still more favourable.

But Mr. MORGAN imputes blame to
the Commissioners for having constantly purchased Stock, except in one
instance, in the three per cents.---
Now, as the 3 per cent. Funds always
bear a greater proportional price than the
Funds which pay a higher rate of Interest, he reproaches the Commissioners
with having laid out the Public Money in
purchasing that Stock which was dearest
in proportion to its real value. What other
reasons the Commissioners might have,
I do not know; but there are three so
obvious, that I am astonished Mr. MOR-

GAN

GAN should not have attended to them. First, that by purchasing that Stock of which the greatest nominal Capital could be bought for the same price, a greater progress would be made towards enabling the Commissioners to pay off the 5 per cents. at par, or, which would probably be more eligible, to reduce the interest of them *: this alone might be much more than equivalent to the making purchases a little more advantageous in the mean time. The second is, that the 4 per cents. forming a much smaller Capital than the 3 per cents. the market would have been much more affected by purchases made in that Stock; and any continuance of purchases in it, would probably have brought up their price to par; and considering merely the interest, the average rates at which the Commissioners have purchased have been equally advantageous

---

* It will be recollected, that these objects are not attainable till 25,000,000l. of the 3 or 4 per cents. shall have been redeemed.

with

with the buying 4 per cents. at par, since
those purchases have, at an average,
scarcely exceeded 75 per cent. The
third reason is, that as the Stock-holders
are not obliged to accept less than 100
per cent. for any species of Stock, it is
the interest of the Public to redeem the
Capital of the Debt while it bears a price
much below par, that they may not be
obliged afterwards to pay for it at par.
Thus, between 1786 and 1792, the 3 per
cents. rose 27 one-half per cent; and
had Peace continued, would in all probability have risen to par; after which I
allow it would have been the business of
the Commissioners to redeem the Stock
which bore the highest rate, unless a bar-
gain had been made for reducing the Interest.

As Mr. MORGAN has taken no notice
of these reasons, I cannot but think the
Commissioners had some better motive
for purchasing 3 per cents. than a wish
" to *appear* to make a progress in dis-
" charging

" charging the Debt, while that progress
" has in fact been retarded."

The single instance in which the Sinking Fund has been applied in purchasing 4 per cents. Mr. MORGAN seems
to consider as something mysterious†;
nothing however can be more easily ex-
plained: It had been found that at these
times when the 3 per cent. Consolidated Annuities were shut, and the Commissioners were consequently under the
necessity of purchasing 3 per cent. Reduced, the price of the latter invariably
rose, as there is always much less of
that Stock on sale, on account of the
smallness of its Capital. This circumstance having been observed, the Commissioners last year, at a time when the
3 per cent. Consols were shut, directed
their purchases to be made in the 4 per
cents. in order to prevent that loss to
the Public which would have arisen

† See Facts, p. 18.

from

from buying the 3 per cent. Reduced at
an advanced price.

As to the omission of reducing the 4
per cents. in 1792, at the time they had
risen to 96, I can only say, that as there
was a general expectation of the continuance of Peace, and of their consequently rising still higher, the Minister seems to
have waited to take advantage of the most
favourable opportunity ; in which he was
certainly guilty of *not foreseeing what* NO-
BODY *foresaw.*

It would be doing great injustice to
Mr. PITT's measures, to omit all mention, as Mr. MORGAN has done, *inad-
vertently no doubt*, of the additional sum of
one per cent. on the Capital of the Stock
created, which, in consequence of an Act
of Parliament proposed by him, is provided in all the new Loans. It required
some hardiness of resolution, to propose
that a Nation so distressed and overbur-
dened as Mr. MORGAN represents this to
be,

be, should expose itself to an additional annual charge, which has actually amounted to 770,000l. in order to avoid entailing their debts upon posterity (see Table IV.) ; and some fertility of resource was necessary, to find the means of raising four millions annually, by additional Taxes, when all the evident objects of taxation seemed exhausted. Nor is less praise due to the regulation by which the produce of the new Taxes is submitted in a distinct and separate form, to the scrutinizing eyes of Parliament, rendering it impossible to confound the new resources with the old, and to conceal deficiencies in a confused mass of Accounts. What the actual produce of the Taxes imposed during the War, has been, I shall have occasion hereafter to state ; but must here make some short remarks on the general system of funding, and the particular plan adopted by Mr. PITT.

Those

Those who contend that a Capital
ought never to be created in funding beyond the sum actually received, do not
sufficiently consider how averse the Lenders would be to advance their Money
upon a Stock which might in the course
be paid off, or reduced. They naturally
require either that their Stock should be
made irredeemable a certain number of
years, or that some other advantage should
be given to them adequate to their risque.
This was found necessary when the Navy
Bills were funded in 5 per cent. Stock in
1784 and 1785, and even with that sti-
pulation, and the little probability that
then appeared of their being ever paid
off, the Holders of the Bills were unwilling to subscribe. It is besides, always
an object with the Money Lenders, to
speculate on the chance of the Funds rising considerably in case of any favourable event, and for this chance they will
often give a consideration more than adequate.

On

On the other hand, the addition of a
large nominal Capital to the National
Debt, is not only discouraging in its appearance, but may prolong the duration
of the Debt, and expose the Public to
the danger of paying, in the course of
Redemption, a much greater sum than
they have received. But without pre-
tending to decide between two such
authorities as Mr. Fox and Mr. Morgan, I shall only observe, that the
extraordinary merit of the system of
funding adopted by the Minister, is
to unite, in a very great degree, the advantages of both ideas. It derives an
advantage from the speculative views of
the Lender, by indulging him with a
Fund at a low rate of Interest, for which
he is willing to give a compensation
rather more than adequate : while on
the other hand, as a greater additional
Capital of Stock is created, the Sinking Fund, which, by a Law passed during the present Administration, must
always bear the same proportion to the
additional

additional Capital created, is increased in an equal degree. Thus, in whatever Fund the Money is borrowed, the time of Redemption, on which Mr. MORGAN lays the greatest stress, is nearly the same.

This mode of funding, in fact, reduces all the Loans lately contracted, to temporary Annuities; the exact duration of which cannot indeed be foreseen, but is circumscribed within certain limits. It would be easy to prove, on this principle, that even if it had been possible to procure Money on 4 per cent. Funds, without sinking their value in the market more than the 3 per cents. were depressed by the Loans raised in them, the advantages of such a system would have been very questionable.

Having ascertained the actual amount of the Expences of the present War, I must observe, that there are two other points of view in which it is very important to consider them. The one is a
com-

comparison of the Expenditure with the force actually exerted; for it is clear, that a sum, moderate in itself, may be lavish and extravagant; and one apparently vast, may be judicious and œconomical, in proportion to the efficacy with which each has been employed. Were Mr. MORGAN's assertions therefore true, that " the Expences of the four first " years of the present War are two-thirds " greater than those of the four first " years of the most extravagant War in " which this Country had ever been en- " gaged;" and that the " Debt incurred " by the present War is more than " double that incurred during the same " period," (both of which assertions, or, as Mr. MORGAN chuses to call them, *facts*, are totally destitute of foundation), still the Administration might deserve the praise of frugality, if the Force they employed was increased in a still greater proportion. I mean therefore to compare the Force employed by Land and Sea, during the four years chosen by Mr.

G MORGAN,

MORGAN, with that which has been maintained during the three last and the present year.

A comparative statement of the Naval Force employed in each of the periods alluded to, will be seen in Table V.; but to form an accurate idea of the improvement of our Fleet, it must also be recollected, that the number of three-decked Ships has been very much increased, and the new Vessels of almost every rate constructed on a much larger scale than formerly. Two new classes of ships have indeed been added to our Navy, that of eighty-gun Ships on two decks, and that of large and powerful Frigates carrying eighteen or twenty-four pounders upon their main decks. And this circumstance I mention the rather, as it must recall to Mr. MORGAN's mind the pleasure which he in common with every other Englishman must feel, in recollecting how many fine Ships of each of these descriptions have been transferred

from

from the Navy of our Enemies to our own.

The increase of the Army has been still more extraordinary, as may be seen also in Table V. ; and in a comparison of Expence, it is particularly to be observed, that the Cavalry have been augmented in a still greater proportion than the Infantry. But exclusive of the addition to the regular Forces of the Kingdom, a defence of a new and unusual kind has been created, in the various Corps of Volunteers, not less important to the preservation of internal tranquillity than to the protection of the Country against a Foreign Invader.

It ought likewise to be considered as a circumstance of great consequence in increasing the necessary Expenditure, that in the present War our Armaments have been rapid beyond all former example. In the American War, we began with a small force, and gradually increased it in

pro-

proportion as the number of our Enemies augmented. In the present instance, the tempest burst suddenly over our heads, and our preservation depended upon immediate exertion. We were called upon to pass instantly from a weak Peace Establishment, to the utmost efforts of our Military and Naval strength.

Having compared the Force employed in the present War with the Charge it has occasioned, I shall proceed to consider that Expence in another point of view, not less important---a comparison with the Expenditure of our Enemies. For when two great Powers are engaged in War, their Expences must necessarily be in some degree proportionate and reciprocal.--- Every exertion on the one part must be opposed by an effort on the other; and though much may be saved by accuracy and economy, it is impossible that the vigour of Military Operations should be increased without a corresponding increase of Expence. I mean therefore to shew,

shew, that in every former War, for more than a Century (as far as I have been able to procure any account), our Expences bore a much larger proportion to those of our Enemies than in the present.

The Naval and Military Expences of King William's War with France, including Ordnance, amounted yearly to about £. 4,227,000

The Expences of the same kind, of Louis XIV. during the same time, to about - 7,690,000

The average Expences of the Succession War, were about - - 5,100,000

Those of Louis XIV. at the same time, about - - - 9,000,000

It must however be observed, that Great Britain was far from holding that distinguished rank in the Alliance against Louis the XIVth, which she maintains in the present Confederacy against the French Republic. The extraordinary Expences of the Dutch in King William's War, exceeded those of England about 150,000l. per annum.

The

The average Expences of the War with
France and Spain, from 1744 to 1748,
were about   -   -   £.8,500,000
The average Expences of the War from
1756 to 1763, were about   -   -   17,770,000
The Expences of France during the same
time, were about   -   -   -   11,100,000
The Expences of the American War were
yearly about   -   -   -   * 23,200,000
Those of France in the same time   -   15,000,000

No accounts are to be met with, at all to be depended upon, of the Expences of Spain, Holland or America: the latter indeed were chiefly defrayed by Paper Money, extremely uncertain in its value.

It is not possible to estimate with any accuracy, the Expences of the French in the present War, as they have also been principally discharged in a paper currency, the value of which cannot be easily ascertained at every period of its emission. But when the immense amount of that Paper Money is considered, and we add to it the vast sums raised by Contributions in the Conquered Countries, and by various modes of plunder and confiscation at home, it will be difficult to suppose the real value of their Expences short of

* See Sir JOHN SINCLAIR's History of the Revenue.

eighty

eighty millions sterling a-year, since the
commencement of the War†. But the
magnitude of the sum expended is a trifling evil, compared with the means by
which it has been raised : the Capital of
a mighty Nation has been thereby nearly
exhausted, its Commerce ruined, its in-

† Le Coulteux estimated, last November, the real
value of all the Assignats then in circulation, to have
amounted, according to the rate of depreciation at the
time of their respective issues, to five milliards, or
upwards of 200 millions sterling ‡. To this must be
added, all the confiscations, both of land and moveables,
the requisitions of cash and effects of every kind, the Dutch
Subsidy, and all the sums extorted in the Netherlands and
Germany ; but those who are inclined to pursue this subject, will find ample and accurate information in Mr.
D'Ivernois' State of the Finances of France.

Since that Estimate was made, the acknowledged amount
of Assignats has been swelled by no less a sum than 20
milliards; a Forced Loan, as far as has been found prac-
ticable, has been carried into effect, which was calculated
to produce 24 millions sterling ; and by the last accounts
received from France, we find, that in the Debate of 23d
February, Dubois de Crance states, that 1500 millions
of livres in specie (about 60 millions sterling), will be
necessary to be raised for the next Campaign, which is
exclusive of the Navy and all other charges.

‡ The nominal value of these Assignats was at least 20 milliards.

dustry

dustry destroyed, and Property within it reduced almost to any empty name.

Having considered the Expences of the War, and the Debt occasioned by them, Mr. MORGAN proceeds to make some *Miscellaneous* Observations, equally accurate and equally consolatory with his remarks on these subjects. He observes, that " from the first establishment of the " Consolidated Fund in 1786, the Ex- " penditure has invariably exceeded the " Revenue." The deficiencies in the six " years preceding the War amounted to " Seven Millions nearly, which were " supplied by Loans and extraordinary " Receipts." For the proof of this, he refers to his Review of Dr. PRICE's Writings (p. 57), where indeed we meet with an extraordinary attempt to shew that the deficiency of the Revenue in five years preceding 1791, amounted to no less than 6,380,000l. This must not a little have astonished the Nation, who had been informed by the Select Committee

mittee (from whose Report Mr. Morgan professes to have taken his mate-
rials), that in these years 4,750,000l. had
been employed in the discharge of the
National Debt, and that the new Debt
amounted only to   -   - £.1,789,589
         viz.

Loan by Tontine in 1789	1,002,140
Ditto by Short Annuities -	187,000
Unfunded Debt of various kinds	600,449

The statement in Table VI. will
immediately explain the mystery ; and
the difference between that statement
and Mr. Morgan's, will be found to arise
merely from my having followed the only
method which he considers as intelligi-
ble and honest.* I have stated the whole
Expenditure of each year separately, and
shewn the sources distinctly from whence
that Expenditure was defrayed : while
Mr. Morgan strikes out of his account
of Income, all those that he calls extraordinary resources, though he inserts
the whole amount of the Expences,

* See Review, &c. p. 63.

H   which

which includes many articles of an occasional and extraordinary nature. If it be said that those sources of income were omitted because they could not be expected to occur again, why is the Lottery excluded, which, whether a wise resource or not, experience has shewn to be very usual, and one which it will be always in the power of Administration to employ.

It is besides not immaterial to notice, that the following temporary and occasional articles are included by Mr. MORGAN, in his account of the ordinary Peace Establishment.

To the American Loyalists	- -	£. 1,336,376
HASTINGS's Trial, Foreign Secret Service, PRINCE's and Civil List Debts, New South Wales, &c.	- -	927,673
Armament in 1787	- - -	253,585
Loan to the STADTHOLDER, deducting what was repaid,	- - -	153,000
Extraordinary Naval Expences, occasioned by the ships put on the stocks, and improvements undertaken in the Dockyards during the American War, in 1786	-	387,000
In this part of the account I cannot pretend to exactness, { 1787	-	414,000
1788	-	189,000
1789	-	172,000
1790	-	276,000
Expence of Fortifications and Buildings by the Ordnance	- - -	222,425

£. 4,331,059

Mr.

(51)

Mr. Morgan gives no statement of the accounts of 1791 and 1792, though he throws out some conjectures concerning them ; but as I entirely agree with him, " that it is wiser to ground our faith on " what *he* has *proved*, than what he has " prophesied," I shall merely again refer to Table VI. which will complete the picture of his Seven Millions Deficiency.

But the succeeding observations are still more alarming ; and as they are in some degree obscure, it is necessary to quote a pretty long passage, that I may not run any risk of misrepresenting Mr. Morgan's meaning, by attempting to abridge it.

" In the last three years, though additional " Taxes have been laid to the amount of four " millions, these deficiencies have constantly " increased, so as in the present year to fall very " little short of two millions. It is probable, " therefore, that Annual Loans will become " necessary in future to provide for the ordinary " Expences of a Peace Establishment; and these " Loans, by requiring new Taxes, will produce " further deficiencies, so that by borrowing each " year, not only to pay the deficiencies of the pre-

H 2   " ceding

" ceding year, but also the interest on the defi-
" ciencies in former years, the National Debt
" will be increasing at Compound Interest in the
" same manner as it is reduced, but with this
" alarming difference, that the operations in the
" one case are ten times more powerful than in
" the other.

" If these are likely to be the effects of the
" Public Debt with the Expenditure only of a
" *Peace* Establishment, or on the supposition
" that the War were immediately closed, what
" must be the consequences of obstinately per-
" sisting in a system of profusion, which, if long
" continued, would ruin any Country, however
" unimpaired its strength and resources.

" That the deficiency in the Revenue pro-
" ceeds chiefly from the distressed and overbur-
" thened state of the Nation, is self-evident:
" but it must also be acknowledged, that it pro-
" ceeds in some degree from the nature of the
" Taxes which have lately been imposed. These,
" in order to render the War less obnoxious,
" have been laid in such a manner as to cause the
" least immediate pressure on the poorer part of
" the people.   Now as this class constitutes the
" great bulk of the Nation, (and if the present
" War continues, is likely to constitute a much.
" greater) it is obvious that a Tax which is not
" immediately paid by them can never be effi-
" cient.   Such Taxes as those for Licences to
" wear Hair-powder, to kill Game, &c. may
" do to fill up the column of Ways and Means
" in a Minister's Budget, but their produce,
" compared with the serious magnitude of
" the

" the public exigencies, must always be trifling
" and contemptible."

It is impossible to read this without
longing for an opportunity to ask Mr.
Morgan where he made all these terrible discoveries ? I cannot but wish he
had at least produced some proof of *facts*
so strange and so important. I am almost afraid to avow, in opposition to so
positive an assertion, that on the authority of every thing I have seen or heard
for these three years, and on that of the
most authentic Statements I have been
able to procure, the whole of this repre-
sentation is entirely false, except one circumstance, which Mr. Morgan, in
kindness to the Minister, has disclosed,
" that the late Taxes have been laid in
such a manner, as to cause the least immediate pressure on the poorer part of
the people." Mr. Morgan indeed ap-
prehends, that this attention has rendered them unproductive, or, in his own
polite phrase, " trifling and contemptible."

I am happy to have it in my power to
console

console Mr. MORGAN, by stating the produce of these *trifling* Taxes, by which it
will appear, that though the poor have
been spared, and the rich, I hope, not
heavily burdened, the public necessities
have been amply provided for. The
same Statements will shew the truth of
Mr. MORGAN's assertion, of the increasing deficiency in the Revenue, and prove
that his Two Millions last year have ex-
actly as much real existence as his Seven
Millions during the Peace. As to the
future Annual Loans, which are, according to Mr. MORGAN, to be contracted
as well in time of Peace as War,
that being matter of *prophecy*, I shall
leave it to the undisturbed possession of
such regard as may be thought due to it.
I must, however, observe, that it is not a
little singular, that Mr. MORGAN should
charge Mr. PITT with imitating the error
of Mr. NECKAR, in France, that of carrying on a War without imposing a new
Tax, by borrowing immense sums annually, and endeavouring to provide for
them by the *ineffectual means of œconomy*.
I hope and believe Mr. PITT is as de-
sirous

sirous as Mr. Neckar of carrying the *means of œconomy* as far as they will go; but with what justice he is charged with imposing no new Taxes, the Public do not need the aid of my statement to judge. Successful would he be, indeed, if all the Nation felt them no more than Mr. Morgan seems to do. But here again it will afford additional satisfaction to look a little back to former times, and recall to memory, that the Taxes imposed during the American War, from 1774 to 1783, produced an annual increase of Revenue of only - - £. 1,755,259 while the Interest of the Debt

contracted in the same period amounted to - - 4,864,000
leaving an annual deficiency
of - - - - 3,108,000

While the Taxes imposed during the present Contest, unparalleled in its dangers, and unequalled in the force exerted by the contending Powers, have not only afforded sufficient to defray the Interest of the sums borrowed, but to discharge,

in

in a period of thirty-nine years, the
Principal of the Debt itself.*

Heated with the subject, Mr. MORGAN
however goes on accumulating debt upon
debt, and calamity on calamity, till he
exclaims " with two Loans in one year,
" amounting to Thirty-six Millions Ster-
" ling; with a Loan also in the same

---

* Comparison of the Interest and Charges of the additions
made to the National Debt since 1786, including 1 per
cent. annually raised to liquidate the Principal of them,
with the produce of the Taxes imposed to answer those
charges in the year ending October 10, 1795.

Years.	£.		£.	Surplus of Taxes.	Defici- ency.
1788. Interest and Charges of Loan by Annuity	59,473	Produce of Taxes	132,885	73,411	—
1793. Interest and Charges of Loan	252,812	Produce of Taxes	226,194	—	26,618
1794. Interest and Charges of Loan	773,324	Produce of Taxes, including the Taxes of 1791 continued	829,876	56,552	—
Feb. 1795. Interest and Charges	1,227,415	Produce of Taxes from Feb. 23 to Oct. 10,	1,040,773		

The Hair Powder Tax, which Mr. MORGAN singles out
as particularly *contemptible*, was taken at 210,000l. and has
produced 208,700l.—The Account laid before the House
of Commons made its produce about 20,000l. less, owing to
some of the returns from the Country not being come in.

" year

" year* to our Ally the Emperor, of
" 4,600,000l. and with an addition to
" the Navy Debt of One Million and an
" Half, the whole Supplies of the next
" Campaign still remain unprovided !"

I have already considered the Loans
and Expences; but it is very odd Mr.
MORGAN should forget, that so early as
page 6, he admitted that the Expences
of the next Campaign *were* provided for.
I certainly cannot promise, nor can the
Minister engage, that the actual Expences may not exceed the Estimates ; but
the Estimates were certainly liberal, and
we have all along been reasoning upon a
supposition that they were sufficient. By
some strange inaccuracy, however, Mr.
MORGAN has so expressed himself, that
his meaning seems to be, that no part of
the Supplies of the next Campaign are

* I am glad, that at least in the conclusion of his Book,
Mr. MORGAN will allow that money to have been *really*
lent to the EMPEROR : for, in all the former Passages in
his work, he has reasoned upon it as a part of our own
Debt.

I   provided

provided for, which he, as well as every body else, must know to be directly contrary to the truth.

Here Mr. Morgan concludes with citing a severe philippic of one of the *best of Patriots*, against a Minister now no more, and new-pointing the thunder of Dr. Price's eloquence against Mr. Pitt's devoted head. This, however, I shall not repeat, because (though I know nothing more of the Nobleman in question, except that I never met with any person acquainted with him during life, who did not love and revere his memory ; yet) I think it equally useless and painful to recall a censure, whether merited or not, of the *dead*, which I have shewn to be totally inapplicable to the *living*, Minister.

But one very material inquiry, perhaps the most material of all, remains behind ---Whether the Expences of the War, however wisely planned, and œconomically
cally

cally executed; are not so great as to ex-
haust in a dangerous degree the resources
of the Nation? Whether we are not
overstraining our sinews, and verging
to a state of faintness and debility, by
exertions beyond our strength?-----I am
far from denying that our exertions have
been great, or from maintaining that
they ought to be continued one moment
longer than that in which they can be
put an end to with safety and honour:
Nor am I disposed to add one to the
number of those adventurous Politicians
who have speculated on the extent and
final term of the National Resources:
But I will point out some obvious
and apparent circumstances, which
convince me that I was not too sanguine
in my opinions two years ago, and that
no efforts hitherto made, are likely to
prove fatal or dangerous to the public
welfare. One circumstance peculiarly
interesting to an Englishman, is the state
of our Navigation and Foreign Trade ;
and in no particular were more destruc-

tive

tive consequences apprehended from the
War. I ventured to contradict those
gloomy apprehensions ; and my utmost
hopes have been more than realized by
the event. Contrary to the examples of
all former Wars (that glorious one only
excepted, which has already shed im-
mortal honours on the name of PITT),
our Commerce has been extended beyond its utmost limits in the most
flourishing years of Peace *, during a
War which has convulsed both the he-
mispheres, and shaken the civilized world
to its center. It will hardly be denied that
a flourishing Trade is at once a cause and
a symptom of National Prosperity, and
History will furnish us with no instance
of a Nation which has extended its commerce abroad, while wealth, industry,
and population decayed at home. But
there are considerations, if possible, still
more decisive. One of the earliest effects
of a contest which in any great degree

* See Table VI.

affects

affects the National Wealth, is to draw
into the coffers of the State that Money
which would otherwise have been employed by individuals in works of public
utility and improvement : In which case
no new enterprizes are undertaken, and
those which have been begun are feebly
carried on, and gradually suspended, generally with the ruin of their undertakers.
All of us who are not very young, must have
remembered how far this effect was produced towards the close of the American
War. The Wars of former times would
furnish us with still more striking examples. But so rapid has been the progress of National Improvement, in the
present times, and so solid is the foundation of General Credit, that they do not
appear to have suffered any material de-
triment from the War, notwithstanding
the increasing pressure of the public burdens, and the extraordinary magnitude
of the projects which had lately been
undertaken. Is needless to prove, that
during the continuance of the late Peace,
. such

such plans had been adopted, of agricultural improvement, of roads and
bridges, of canals, of extended buildings
in almost all our Provincial Cities, and
of additions to London alone equal to
many Cities; as far exceeded the utmost
limits of imagination in times past. But
the execution of these projects has suffered so little interruption from the exigencies of the times, that many others
of not less hardy conception have been
undertaken during the War itself †.

† The number of Navigation Bills passed in the last six
years of peace and prosperity; with the amount of the
money subscribed, and allowed to be raised in addition to
the subscriptions, will appear by the following Statement,
as well as those which have passed since the commencement of the War:

YEARS OF PEACE.				WAR.		
	No.	Subscription. £.	Allowed beyond Subscription. £.		No. Subscriptions. £.	Allowed beyond Subscription. £.
1787	—	—	—			
1788	3	70,600	65,000			
1789	3	86,000	50,000			
1790	4	286,300	86,000	1793	22 2,207,160	727,600
1791	10	532,000	305,000	1794	16 2,039,500	666,000
1792	9	710,100	373,500	1795	9 283,900	185,000

Total of 6 yrs. 29 1,684,400 879,500 Total of 3 yrs. 47 4,530,500 1,578,600
Number of Inclosure Bills passed in   Number of Inclosure Bills passed in
the same six years, - 210   the same three years, - 217

And

And so little has Money been found wanting for the execution of profitable undertakings, that at this time the first of our Corporations is engaged in an eager contest with a Body of Individuals, to decide which party shall be permitted to expend no less a sum than 800,000l. upon a project, the success of which must depend totally on the extension of the Trade of London ‡.

Another criterion not less important, may be derived from the produce of the internal Taxes, which falling on almost every article of consumption, excepting these of immediate and absolute necessity, furnish a pretty certain indication

‡ That the increase of Trade in the second Port in England has kept pace with that in the first, will sufficiently appear from the following comparison of the number of Ships which have paid the Dock-duties at Liverpool in different years:

	Number of Ships.	Amount of Duties.
Average of the years 1752 to 1755 inclusive, -	No account.	£. 2053
Average of the years 1773 to 1775 inclusive, - -	2254	5229
Average of the years 1783 to 1792 inclusive, - -	3418	8928
Average of the years 1793 to 1795 inclusive, -	4114	10,842

of

of the comforts or necessities of the People. Accordingly it has always been found, that when the burdens of the State bore heavily on the Nation, the income of these Taxes gradually declined, and that effect has been considered as so constant during War, as scarcely to afford any reason for apprehension, because it was supposed it would recover of itself after the return of Peace. ...But if during the present War, their produce has scarcely diminished, notwithstanding the great additions made to them, it affords a most extraordinary proof that the general mass of National Property has increased to a degree not only capable of bearing its former burdens, but of supporting so great an additional weight, without injuring the happiness of the People †.

† I have before had occasion to state the produce of the Permanent Taxes to the commencement of the War.

In 1793 it amounted to 13,953,000l.
    1794 - - 13,827,000l.
    1795 - - 13,418,727l.

A very productive branch of Revenue was cut off in 1795, by the stoppage of the Distilleries, which would account for a greater diminution.

Mr.

Mr. MORGAN has indeed, in his improved Edition, disclosed the secret of
this extraordinary produce of the Taxes.
He tells us (p. 48), " it is obvious, that
" the greater the profusion of Public
" Money, the greater must be the pro-
" duce of the Public Revenue. In the
" present War, which exceeds all that
" ever preceded it in the enormity of its
" Expence, the Revenue must of course
" be increased in a higher degree than in
" any other War, and consequently
" whenever it terminates, the deficiency
" must be so much the more alarming."
This is a reason for continuing the War,
which its *warmest advocates* certainly never thought of. A discovery concealed
from the ignorant Ministers, the CECILS
and the SULLYS of former times, and re-
served for the enlightened Statesmen of
Dr. PRICE's School. If the Excise and
Customs sunk a third before the Peace of
Ryswick, it was because the Wars in
Flanders and Ireland were not sufficiently expensive ; if the Taxes declined

K   in

in the American War, it was only because the Ministry were too œconomical. But by what strange accident can
it have happened, that though the Rulers
of the French Republic have spent
twenty millions a year for their Civil
List, and sixty for the War, yet the
Taxes in France have scarce produced any thing at all? I hope Mr.
MORGAN will tell us in his next improved Edition, whether they have been
too frugal. As he " feels no pleasure
in anticipating evil," I almost wish he
had left us under the happy delusion,
that the return of Peace would be as favourable to the Public Revenue as to the
property acquired by private industry.

Mr. MORGAN is indeed so sceptical, with
regard to the Property of the Nation *, as
to estimate the Rental of England at only
eighteen millions. For this statement he
gives us no proof, except the very strange
one, that the Land-Tax charged not

* Facts, p. 24.

only

only on lands and houses, but also on the *growing produce of the Place and Pension List*, produces about 1,900,000l. a year. Can it possibly be necessary to inform Mr. MORGAN, or can he possibly suppose his Readers ignorant, that the Land-Tax is assessed according to an invariable rate established above a century ago? It is well known to have been so unequally distributed at first, as to afford no adequate criterion of the Property of the Nation even at that time; and has not been changed at all on account of any improvements since. But Mr. MORGAN's hint respecting *Places and Pensions*, makes it not improper to remind him that the reduction of the Pension List, and the abolition of useless Places under the present Administration, far exceeds the amount of any increase of Offices which the necessity of the Public Service has required during the same period: and that even some of those Offices will be found, on inquiry, to have produced a diminution of

influence,

influence, and saving of expence, which, of itself, much more than counterbalances the charge brought on the Public*.

The

* All the Provisions, and Stores of every kind, which used to be furnished by Contract, or on Commission, by various Persons, are now purchased by the Commissioners of the Victualling, and the Commissioners for Transports. The amount of Sums paid to Individuals for such Services from 1778 to 1783, was upwards of 17,000,000l.

Offices abolished under the Civil List Act.

	No.	£.
Above the value of £. 500 per Annum	37	43,600
Under ditto	97	13,900
	134	£. 57,500

Offices abolished under Treasury Regulations.

	No.	£.
Above the value of £. 500 per Annum	3	2,156
Under ditto	141	11,469
	144	£. 13,625

Offices substituted in lieu of those abolished.

	No.	£.
Above the value of £. 500 per Annum	5	3,538
Under ditto	57	7,371
	62	£. 10,909

	No.	Annual Value.
Number of Offices suppressed	278	£. 71,125
Ditto substituted	62	10,909
	216	£. 60,216
Savings by Exchequer Offices		£. 25,000
Ditto by Auditors of Imprests		32,000
		£. 57,000

Sinecure

The Estimates of the celebrated GRE-
GORY KING, make the Rental of the Nation, about the time the Land-Tax was
imposed, 13 millions, at the following
Rates, viz.

Arable Land,	£.o	5	6 per Acre.
Pasture and Meadow,	,o,	8	8
Woods and Coppices,	o	5	o
Forests, Parks and Commons,	o	3	8
Heaths, Moors, &c.	o	1	o

Let those who are acquainted with
the value of Land in the present day, decide whether the Chancellor of the Ex-

Sinecure Offices in Customs, held by persons not resident,
which have been suppressed by Mr. PITT as the Pos-
sessors have died.

	No.	Annual Value.
Vacant	40	£.11,000
To fall in	84	38,000
	124	£.49,000

Reduction of Excise Officers since 1783.

765 reduced - £.12,345
300 added for Tobacco, &c.

465

Pensions reduced since 1783.
£.30,000 a Year.

chequer

chequer overstated the actual Rental of
England at twenty-five millions, even
making no allowance for the vast tracts
of Land which have either been recovered
from the Waste, or brought into improved cultivation, within this Century.
About the same time I have been speaking of, DAVENANT computed the Rental of this Kingdom to have increased
since the year 1600, from six millions to
at least fourteen ; and I scarcely need
observe, that in all the visible tokens of
public improvements, the present Century has greatly excelled the last. I
knew no more than Mr. MORGAN, on
what grounds Mr. PITT estimated the
Personal Property of the Nation ; but
believing, for the reasons I have men-
tioned, that he very wisely kept much
within the truth in valuing the Land,
and having seen Estimates which appear to me judicious and reasonable, and
which much exceed the amount he men-
tioned, am persuaded that in the other
instance

instance he was not less moderate and cautious.

It might also be proper to inquire into the state of Public Credit, but having already had occasion to discuss that subject, in speaking of the Loans contracted during the War, I shall make no farther mention of it here.

Of the general mass of Income which the People, collectively considered, derive either from their industry or their possessions, a certain part is employed in supplying them with the necessaries of life. Upon this no part of the burdens of the State can fall, except in Governments of grievous tyranny, such as a short time ago existed (if it does not still exist), in France. And even in that case, they cannot fall upon the income so employed, till they have nearly exhausted that which was appropriated to any other purpose.

Another

(72)

Another part furnishes the conveniencies and comforts of the individuals, and affords their luxuries of whatever nature, whether more or less refined. On this part, the great bulk of the taxes in this Nation falls; and it must give the greatest satisfaction to every friend of his Country, to observe, that notwithstanding the increase of the Public Charges, the use of such articles as fall under this description has not diminished*.

* The assessed Taxes on Carriages, Horses, Servants, &c. apply to the articles which are most generally considered as Luxuries; I shall therefore give a statement of the Assessed Taxes since the commencement of the War, not including any of the New Duties.

	1793.	1794.	1795.
Houses and Windows, including Commutation	1,048,918	1,058,256	1,066,754
Male Servants	92,856	92,900	92,155
Horses	110,132	109,656	110,349
Carriages	187,641	188,899	192,559
Ten per Cent.	91,602	92,200	93,227
	£.1,531,149	1,541,911	1,555,044

A third

A third part of the general Income is employed in procuring comforts of a substantial and permanent nature, as buildings and furniture ; and in these the appearance of the country furnishes no proof of decay. It is true, that some undertakings of this kind have been suspended, but they will be commonly found to be such as had been attempted on too adventurous a speculation.

Another mode in which the Income of the Nation is employed, is to replace, and in favourable times to increase, the Capital vested in Trade. And here, instead of any diminution, the Table of Exports and Imports will furnish decisive proofs of a rapid increase ; for it is impossible for Trade to extend without an augmentation either of actual Capital, or, which is equally a proof of National Prosperity, of solid and substantial Credit.

The last employment of Income I shall take notice of, is in undertakings which

facilitate

facilitate the general intercourse of the
Country, and augment the means of rendering it productive, and of turning the
industry of the People to advantage. In
this class may be placed, the Inclosure of
Wastes, the formation of Manufacturing
Establishments, and the Improvement of
Roads, Harbours and Canals. And these
are works of permanent advantage, ex-
tending the blessings of trade and plenty
to future generations. By Undertakings
like these, I have shewn the present War
(formidable as it really is, and *disastrous*
as it has been represented), to have been
distinguished beyond the most flourishing
years of Peace.

From all these circumstances, I cannot avoid drawing the conclusion, that
amidst all the alarms and difficulties of
so terrible a warfare, the prosperity of
the Country has not materially suffered,
however we may regret the necessity
which forced us unavoidably into the
contest, and now compels us to the continuance

tinuance of it. But surely it will ever be remembered among the most signal blessings which have attended this favoured Isle, that in a time like the present, we are able to look for Peace with confidence, or for War without alarm. History will record the events of the struggle in which Great Britain has repelled the gigantic efforts of the Modern Vandals, armed with all the arts of destruction, and inflamed with the spirit of universal desolation. And future Statesmen will investigate the causes which enabled her, without exhausting her ordinary resources, to withstand an Enemy, who, casting away every idea of self-preservation, consumed his own vitals in his efforts to annoy the Foe.

FINIS.

www.ingramcontent.com/pod-product-compliance
Lightning Source LLC
Chambersburg PA
CBHW020333090426
42735CB00009B/1522